Published in 2014 by The Rosen Publishing Group, Inc.
29 East 21st Street, New York, NY 10010

Photo Credits: **KEY** tl=top left; tc=top center; tr=top right; cl=center left; c=center; cr=center right; bl=bottom left; br=bottom right; bg=background
CBT = Corbis; DT = Dreamstime; iS = istockphoto.com; MP = Minden Pictures; SH = Shutterstock; wiki = Wikipedia

6–7tc wiki; **10**bl CBT; tl DT; br, c SH; **15**br, cl, tr iS; **26**br DT; cr, tc iS; c SH; **26**bg iS; **28**c DT; cr iS; tr SH; **28–29**bg SH; **29**tr MP; **30**br iS; **30–31**bg SH

All illustrations copyright Weldon Owen Pty Ltd, except **1**c, **24**br, **29**bl Magic Group

Weldon Owen Pty Ltd
Managing Director: Kay Scarlett
Creative Director: Sue Burk
Publisher: Helen Bateman
Senior Vice President, International Sales: Stuart Laurence
Vice President Sales North America: Ellen Towell
Administration Manager, International Sales: Kristine Ravn

Library of Congress Cataloging-in-Publication Data

Stephens, David, 1945–
 Coastal habitats / by David Stephens.
    pages cm. — (Discovery education: Habitats)
Includes index.
 ISBN 978-1-4777-1321-1 (library binding) — ISBN 978-1-4777-1477-5 (paperback) — ISBN 978-1-4777-1478-2 (6-pack)
1. Coastal ecology—Juvenile literature. I. Title.
 QH541.5.C65S74 2014
 577.5′1—dc23
                            2012043670

Manufactured in the United States of America

CPSIA Compliance Information: Batch #S13PK3: For Further Information contact Rosen Publishing, New York, New York at 1-800-237-9932

Discovery
EDUCATION™

HABITATS

COASTAL HABITATS

DAVID STEPHENS

PowerKiDS
press™

New York

Contents

The Coastline

Wherever oceans meet land, the actions of waves, currents, and tides, helped by wind and rain, work together to shape the coastline. Rising sea levels and storm surges, which are intensified by global warming, threaten to take away large sections of coastal land. One thing is certain: the coastline is always changing.

The Twelve Apostles
Limestone sea stacks, some as high as 150 feet (46 m), create a spectacular coastline in southern Australia.

Coastal landforms

Waves and tides cut into rocky coastlines to form cliffs, caves, arches, and stacks. Ocean currents dump sand to create sandbars, spits, and beaches.

River delta
Rock and mud flow from upstream and are deposited in the mouth of the river.

Lagoon
This is a bay that has become enclosed by a sandbar.

Tombolo
An island slows the action of waves. Sand is deposited, joining the island to the mainland.

Barrier island
This is formed by a buildup of sand between two tidal inlets.

Making a sea stack
Sea stacks start as the tip of a headland or steep cliff. Then, waves start to erode the base of the cliff.

Sea cave
Pounding waves eat away at the cliff and make a cave entrance.

Sea arch
The waves eventually cut a hole through the headland.

Sea stack
The top of the arch falls into the sea, leaving a sea stack.

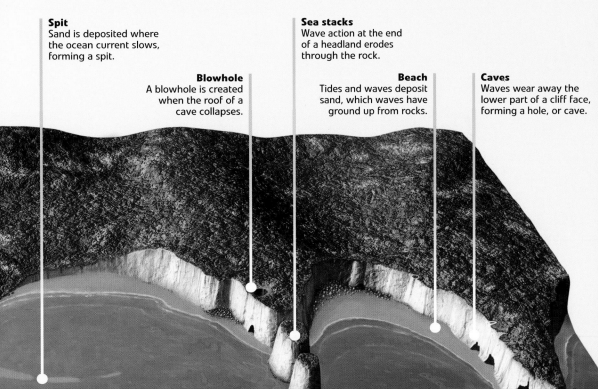

Spit
Sand is deposited where the ocean current slows, forming a spit.

Sea stacks
Wave action at the end of a headland erodes through the rock.

Blowhole
A blowhole is created when the roof of a cave collapses.

Beach
Tides and waves deposit sand, which waves have ground up from rocks.

Caves
Waves wear away the lower part of a cliff face, forming a hole, or cave.

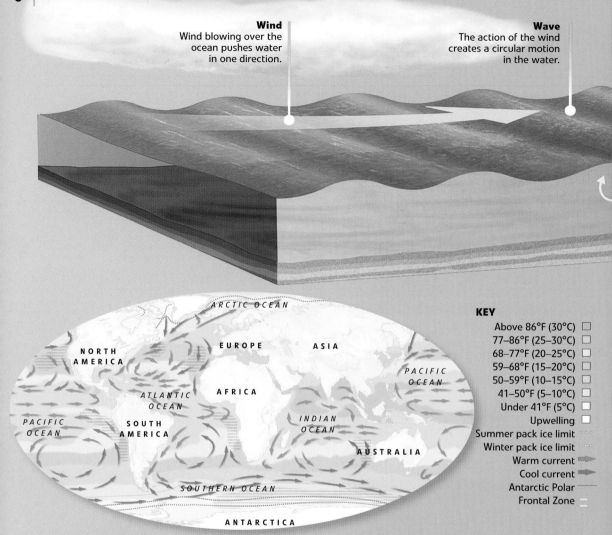

Wind
Wind blowing over the ocean pushes water in one direction.

Wave
The action of the wind creates a circular motion in the water.

ARCTIC OCEAN

NORTH AMERICA

EUROPE

ASIA

PACIFIC OCEAN

ATLANTIC OCEAN

AFRICA

PACIFIC OCEAN

SOUTH AMERICA

INDIAN OCEAN

AUSTRALIA

SOUTHERN OCEAN

ANTARCTICA

KEY

Above 86°F (30°C)	☐
77–86°F (25–30°C)	☐
68–77°F (20–25°C)	☐
59–68°F (15–20°C)	☐
50–59°F (10–15°C)	☐
41–50°F (5–10°C)	☐
Under 41°F (5°C)	☐
Upwelling	☐
Summer pack ice limit	···
Winter pack ice limit	···
Warm current	→
Cool current	→
Antarctic Polar Frontal Zone	═

Waves, Tides, and Currents

A little more than 70 percent of Earth's surface is covered by oceans—water that is always moving. Earth rotates once every 24 hours. The force of gravity from the Sun and Moon pulls the water, making it bulge on both sides of Earth. This creates two high and two low tides every day. Earth's rotation and the action of wind on the ocean surface create currents. Tides, wind, and ocean currents make waves.

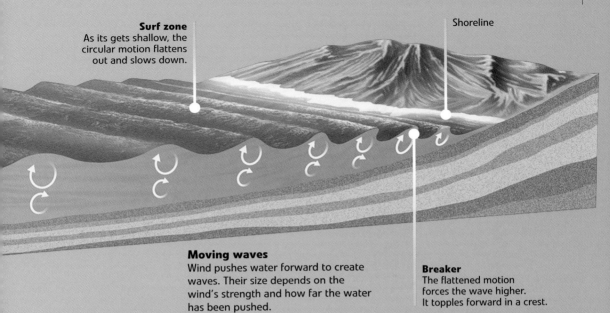

Surf zone
As its gets shallow, the circular motion flattens out and slows down.

Shoreline

Moving waves
Wind pushes water forward to create waves. Their size depends on the wind's strength and how far the water has been pushed.

Breaker
The flattened motion forces the wave higher. It topples forward in a crest.

Ocean currents
Currents flow clockwise in the Northern Hemisphere and counterclockwise in the Southern Hemisphere. Currents help balance temperatures around Earth.

OCEAN TIDES

The effect of gravity on the Sun, Moon, and Earth causes the oceans to bulge on the side of Earth that faces the Moon and on the opposite side.

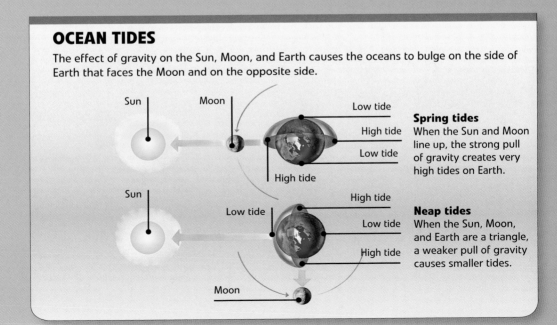

Sun   Moon   Low tide
High tide
Low tide
High tide

Spring tides
When the Sun and Moon line up, the strong pull of gravity creates very high tides on Earth.

Sun   High tide
Low tide   Low tide
High tide
Moon

Neap tides
When the Sun, Moon, and Earth are a triangle, a weaker pull of gravity causes smaller tides.

Beach

Foredunes

Beach zones

The beach is above and below the low-tide mark. During storms, the foredunes lose sand, which is deposited closer to the water. When the storm is over, normal wind and wave action flatten out the beach and build up the foredunes again. Vegetation on secondary dunes traps blowing sand and stabilizes the foredunes. The maritime forest has salt-resistant plants.

Clams

A clam has a hinged shell that protects its soft body. It has a single foot to dig burrows in the wet sand. Its strawlike siphon filters tiny food particles from seawater.

Horned ghost crab

This crab burrows above the high-water mark in the day, then feeds at night. It has body cavities that collect water from the damp sand and pass it through its gills.

Amphipods

These tiny relatives of the shrimp family are about the size of your fingernail and are found in all water environments. They mostly hunt for food at the water's edge.

Oystercatchers

These birds are found worldwide, wading in rock pools and on the water's edge. They eat beach worms and shellfish, which they pry open with their long beaks.

Secondary dunes

Maritime forest

Sandy Shores

Beaches can be made of rocks, pebbles, mud, or sand. Sand is ground-up particles of different substances, ranging in color from white (ground-up coral) to black (tiny particles of lava). Unlike rocky cliffs that wear away over time, beaches can repair themselves after a heavy attack from the sea. Beaches show few signs of life except for crabs and seabirds, but dig down and there are worms, clams, shrimp, and other small creatures hiding in the sand.

Kelp Forests

I n the shallows off many rocky shorelines, towering forests of kelp—a type of seaweed—grow. Kelp forests occur throughout the world, from polar regions to the tropics. These rich aquatic habitats are home to many sea creatures. Some nibble on the kelp, while others feed on the millions of plankton. Larger marine animals hunt the plentiful supply of fish that live there.

FOOD CHAIN OF THE KELP FOREST

Hundreds of sea creatures depend on kelp forests for food and a safe place to live. These forests are vital to the environment.

1 Kelp soaks up sunlight for photosynthesis. The kelp forest grows.

2 A sea snail nibbles the kelp.

3 A lobster eats the sea snail.

4 A shark eats the lobster.

5 After the shark dies, a crab feeds on its remains.

Sea urchin

These slow-moving creatures live on algae that they find in the kelp forest. Their spiny exteriors help protect them from some predators, but the purple sea urchin is still the sea otter's favorite food.

California sea lion

The sea lion feeds mainly on squid and fish from the kelp forest. It closes its nose to hold its breath and stay underwater for up to 15 minutes. Some sea lions swim 200 miles (320 km) upriver for salmon.

Sea otter

This small marine mammal was once hunted almost to extinction because of its thick, soft fur. Its ability to use rocks to break open shellfish and sea urchins so it can eat the soft food inside is rare among sea mammals.

Sea star

There are 2,000 species of starfish or sea stars in the world's oceans. Most have five legs but some species have six. They can regrow a leg that is lost to a predator.

Garibaldi damselfish

These vivid orange fish nest among the kelp and gather algae to feed their young. They are named after an Italian hero, Giuseppe Garibaldi, who always wore a bright-colored shirt.

Orca

Orcas, or killer whales, grow to 26 feet (8 m) and are at the top of the ocean's food chain. They hunt for seals, sea otters, and fish in the kelp forest and even attack sharks and other whales, too.

The kelp forest

Kelp is a plant, so it needs sunlight. It can grow up to 20 inches (50 cm) in a day. Some kelp plants grow as high as a 13-story building.

Rocky Shores

Pounding waves shape the rocky parts of the coast into different environments. In some places, strange and spectacular rock formations develop, such as massive cliffs and caves, rock arches and sea stacks, and blowholes. Sometimes, the erosion is on a small scale, wearing away holes in rocky crevices, which make ideal nesting sites for seabirds. The rocky shore is harsh, and living there is tough. Only the strongest plants and animals survive. Most creatures seek out sheltered areas, where they are protected from the strong winds and constant salt spray.

Gulls
These nest on the ground in large, noisy colonies.

Living on the edge

Rocky coastlines are home to thousands of seabirds. Some nest on the cliffs. Others use the grassy headlands. The albatross and some other seabirds come to shore only once a year to breed.

Tufted puffins
With their strong beaks, these birds dig burrow nests.

Blowhole
Waves crash into the mouth of a sea cave and shoot skyward through a hole in the roof, as at the Nakalele blowhole in Hawaii.

Lighthouses
These buildings warn mariners of dangerous coastlines. Lighthouse keepers kept the lamps burning, but now they are no longer manned.

Weathering
The physical and chemical shaping of rocks is done by water in its different forms of rain, ice, and surf. It can result in unusual formations.

Rock Pools

H oles in the rocky shoreline are covered with water at high tide, then exposed when the tide goes out. These rock pools are a good place to observe marine life. Small fish and crabs hide under the seaweed. Starfish and anemones cling to the rock walls, along with mussels and oysters. Occasionally, a small octopus may be lurking, but watch out for the blue-ringed octopus. This 7-inch (18 cm) octopus is one of the world's most venomous creatures. It has enough toxin to kill 26 adults in only a few minutes.

Hermit crab

THE LIFE CYCLE OF A MUSSEL

A mussel starts life as a tiny larva that swims around for a few weeks before settling on a rock or a jetty pylon, usually in the intertidal zone. It grows a hinged shell attached by fine threads. It sucks in seawater with its strawlike siphon and filters out microscopic sea creatures to feed on.

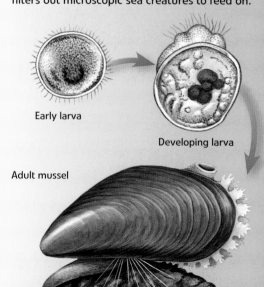

Early larva

Developing larva

Adult mussel

Inside a starfish
Tubes inside a starfish pump water in and out of its tube feet. As the water pressure builds, the feet bend and the starfish moves forward. Many species have a special stomach that pushes out of the body, surrounds and digests prey, then draws the remains back into its body.

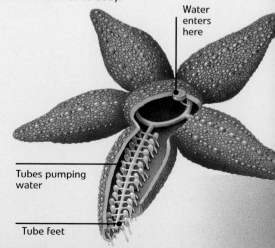

Water enters here

Tubes pumping water

Tube feet

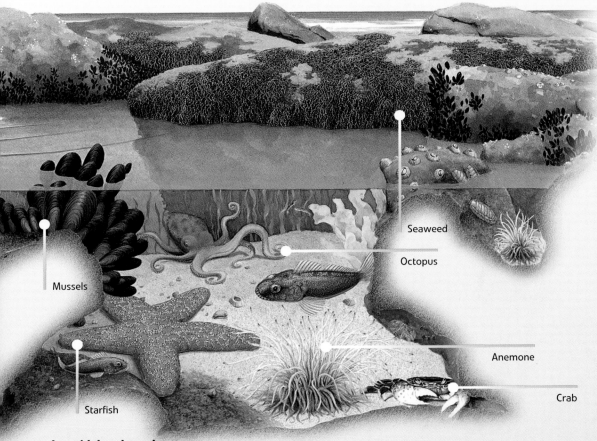

Seaweed

Octopus

Mussels

Anemone

Crab

Starfish

In a tidal rock pool
The water temperature, salinity, and oxygen content are always changing in a tidal rock pool. Huge waves crash in at high tide, then there are the hot sun and predators at low tide.

Subtidal zone
This zone is exposed when the tide is very low. Brown kelp and red seaweed grow here.

Splash zone
Waves splash this area but the tide does not cover it. Blue-green algae cling to rocks here.

Intertidal zone
The area between the high-tide and low-tide mark supports bright green seaweed.

Rock pool

Rocky shoreline
The zones of the rocky shoreline support different algae species. Rock pools have the greatest number of varieties.

Estuaries

An estuary is the border between the freshwater of a river and the tidal salt water of the sea. Mud carried downstream by the river mixes with sand washed in by the tides. This creates fertile areas of land called deltas. Mangrove forests spring up and their roots provide a sheltered breeding ground for marine animals. They attract many species of wading birds looking for food. Even humans like the easy fishing of the estuary.

Life in an estuary

Protected waters in an estuary with mangroves make a perfect breeding ground and nursery for fish and other marine life.

Great egret
The egret stabs at fish, shrimp, and even small reptiles.

Avocet
With its long, curved bill, this bird sifts the mud for insects and shrimp.

Bluefish
Young bluefish look for a meal of shrimp and small fish.

Blue crab
The female spawns millions of eggs in protected waters.

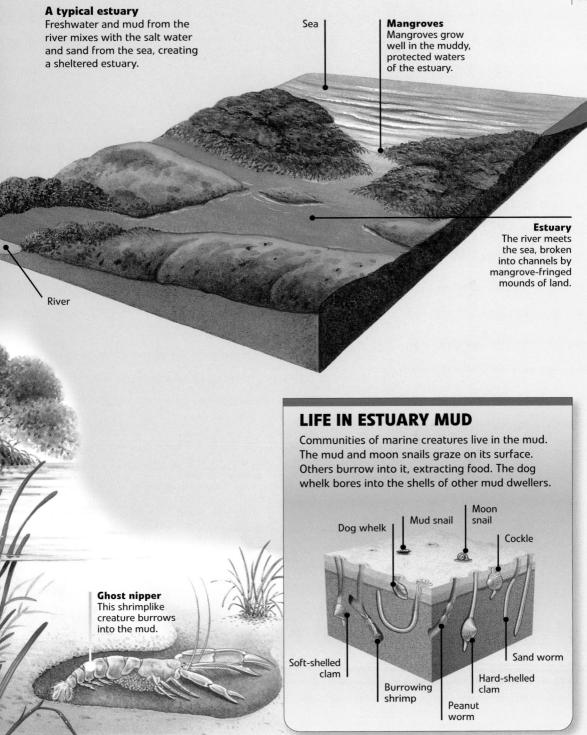

A typical estuary
Freshwater and mud from the river mixes with the salt water and sand from the sea, creating a sheltered estuary.

Sea

Mangroves
Mangroves grow well in the muddy, protected waters of the estuary.

Estuary
The river meets the sea, broken into channels by mangrove-fringed mounds of land.

River

LIFE IN ESTUARY MUD

Communities of marine creatures live in the mud. The mud and moon snails graze on its surface. Others burrow into it, extracting food. The dog whelk bores into the shells of other mud dwellers.

Dog whelk

Mud snail

Moon snail

Cockle

Soft-shelled clam

Burrowing shrimp

Peanut worm

Hard-shelled clam

Sand worm

Ghost nipper
This shrimplike creature burrows into the mud.

Coral reefs of the world
Most coral reefs are found in warm tropical waters at shallow depths, although there are a few reefs growing in cold waters or deep waters.

KEY
☐ Warm ocean
■ Deep-water coral reefs
☐ Warm-water coral reefs

Coral Reefs

A coral reef is a huge, living organism that provides a protective home for thousands of brightly colored fish and other marine animals. A reef is built over thousands of years by millions of simple animals called polyps. A polyp has a soft, tubelike body and a mouth ringed by stinging tentacles. As it grows, it leaves behind limestone (calcium carbonate) that it has extracted from the seawater. The limestone from millions of tiny polyps fuse together and leave behind the beautiful coral reef.

Fan coral
Each stem of a fan coral is covered in hundreds of polyps.

Bubble coral
The white bubbles expand in the day to collect sunlight.

Coral communities
A coral reef is beautiful but fragile, full of soft and hard corals, fish, starfish, mollusks, and sponges. Unfortunately, every year, large areas of reef are damaged by human activities.

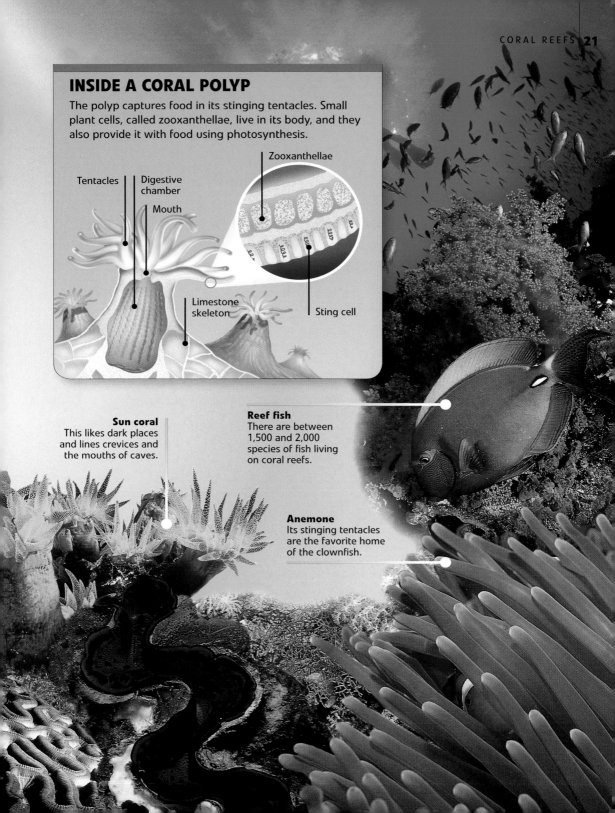

INSIDE A CORAL POLYP

The polyp captures food in its stinging tentacles. Small plant cells, called zooxanthellae, live in its body, and they also provide it with food using photosynthesis.

Zooxanthellae

Tentacles

Digestive chamber

Mouth

Limestone skeleton

Sting cell

Sun coral
This likes dark places and lines crevices and the mouths of caves.

Reef fish
There are between 1,500 and 2,000 species of fish living on coral reefs.

Anemone
Its stinging tentacles are the favorite home of the clownfish.

Shorebirds

Craggy coastlines, muddy estuaries, tropical atolls, salt marshes, swamps, and sandy or pebbly beaches—all these places attract birds. Food is plentiful and the weather is more temperate than at sea. These are ideal conditions for nesting and breeding. Different birds have adapted to their preferred environment, and each nest is a masterpiece of design, camouflage, and protection for the newborn.

Atlantic puffin
This bird hunts far out in the North Atlantic and carries fish back in its large bill for its young.

Common guillemot (murre)

Black guillemot

Shorebird habitat
The many shorebird habitats along the world's coastlines are under threat from humans.

Guillemots
These fly very fast and low over the sea and swim, sometimes in groups, in inshore waters.

Cory's shearwater

Black-bellied plover

Pied avocet

Northern gannet

Great cormorant

Eurasian curlew

Little tern

Ring-billed gull
Its yellow bill has a black ring around the tip. Its nest is a scrape in the ground, padded with grass.

Arctic tern
This small bird migrates 44,300 miles (71,300 km) a year, from the Arctic to the Antarctic and back again.

Avocet
This wading bird lives in many estuaries and wetlands. It nests on the ground in large colonies.

Gulls
At least 45 different gull species feed mostly close to shore. They are expert scavengers.

Yellow-legged gull

Mew gull

Juvenile herring gull

Herring gull

SOOTY TERN
The sooty tern has developed a unique way to stop its egg from drying out so that the chick inside can grow without cracking the shell.

1 Wets its belly on the waves.

2 Returns wet to the nest.

3 Drips water on the egg.

1 The booby begins its steep dive.

DIVING FOR FISH

When it spots a school of anchovies or sardines, this booby dives from about 100 feet (30 m) high to hit the water at 60 miles per hour (97 km/h). Special air sacs under the skin of its face soften the impact. The booby dives after the fish, eating what it can.

2 Its wings fold into a dart shape.

3 Air sacs cushion the high-speed impact.

Turtles
Turtles are slow on land but swim fast. They must surface to breathe, which makes them easy targets for sharks.

Coastal Creatures

Shallow coastal waters are home to a wide selection of marine creatures. This is because of the sunlight that can penetrate these waters. It lets the seaweed and kelp grow and produce food through photosynthesis—just like other plants. They are the basis of an entire food chain. Tiny marine creatures called plankton thrive in the warm, sunlit waters and feed on the seaweed. Fish and crustaceans eat the plankton and algae. Larger creatures, such as turtles and rays, feed on the smaller fish and plants. At the top of the food chain, there are the ever-present sharks.

African red knob sea star
This sea star of the Indian Ocean feeds on algae when young. But when it grows larger, it eats everything from coral to crustaceans.

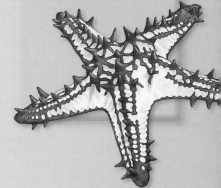

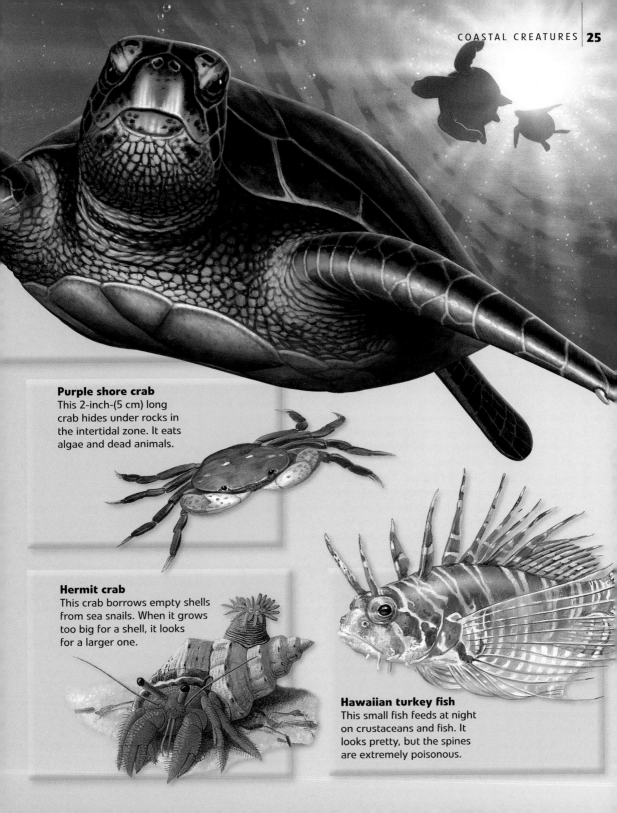

Purple shore crab
This 2-inch-(5 cm) long crab hides under rocks in the intertidal zone. It eats algae and dead animals.

Hermit crab
This crab borrows empty shells from sea snails. When it grows too big for a shell, it looks for a larger one.

Hawaiian turkey fish
This small fish feeds at night on crustaceans and fish. It looks pretty, but the spines are extremely poisonous.

Coral bleaching

When coral becomes stressed due to high water temperatures and other reasons, the zooxanthellae, which live in the coral polyps and provide most of the polyps' food, die off. As a result, the coral loses its color. This is coral bleaching.

Crown-of-thorns

This starfish feeds on coral. The coral regrows when only a few starfish eat it, but it cannot cope with a crown-of-thorns outbreak. Scientists think the outbreaks are caused by water pollution and overfishing of predators such as the Maori wrasse.

Oil pollution

Scientists estimate that about 706 million gallons (2,673 million l) of oil leak into the ocean every year. More than half the oil comes from storm water drains or waste oil disposal from industries. The oil creates havoc with the bird and marine life of the coast.

Rising sea levels

Global warming causes sea levels to rise. This is because warmer water takes up more space than colder water, so sea levels rise. In the last 100 years, sea levels have risen by about 8 inches (20 cm). This causes more storm surges, coastal flooding, and erosion.

Beach pollution

Plastic bags, bottles, fishing tackle, and other trash can trap and kill wildlife and also spoil the beach environment. Disposing of trash properly helps keep the beach clean.

Under Threat

The world's oceans and coastlines are under pressure from human activities. Many oceans are overfished by massive factory ships with huge nets. Oil spills from offshore wells and tankers have a devastating effect on habitats and wildlife. Scientists also believe that sea levels and sea temperatures are rising because of global warming.

Fact File

Exploring the water's edge uncovers many interesting, unusual, and even puzzling sea creatures. There are also spectacular rock formations and habitats ranging from wetlands to cliffs. Next time you visit the coast, keep your eyes open for all the wonders the shoreline has to offer.

Black sand beach

Different kinds of beaches

A sand beach is made of rock that has been ground into particles by waves. It gets its color from the original rock. If the rock was black volcanic basalt, the beach will be black sand. A white or pink beach comes from coral.

Gray sand beach

Pelicans

The lower part of a pelican's bill can hold up to 3 gallons (11 l) of water. This is two to three times more than its stomach can hold.

White sand beach

Brown pelican

Herring gull

Why do gulls stand on one leg?

Standing on one leg is typical resting behavior for most shorebirds, including gulls. They tuck the other leg under one wing to keep it warm. During cold weather, they also tuck their heads under a wing so they do not lose body heat from it.

THICK-BILLED MURRES

These birds lay one egg at a time on bare, coastal rock ledges. While most eggs are oval in shape, this egg is pear-shaped so it will only roll around and not roll off the cliff.

Murre with egg

Pear-shaped egg

Sea anemones

These animals with stinging tentacles reproduce by splitting into two. Each half becomes a new animal. Some fish are not affected by the stings of the tentacles and make their home among them to keep safe from predators.

Stranded

When 80 pilot whales stranded themselves on Tokerau Beach in New Zealand, local people tried to refloat them. Fortunately, a pod of dolphins that had been catching fish out at sea arrived in the shallows. They swam around the whales and guided them back out to sea, saving 76 of the whales.

Colonial sea squirt

Bottlenose dolphin

Sea squirts

The sea squirt is often mistaken for a plant. It is an animal, and it has been on Earth for between 500 and 600 million years. To get food, a 1-inch (2.5 cm) sea squirt filters about 1 quart (1 l) of seawater every hour. This helps keep the waters of the reef clean.

Be a Marine Biologist

Next time you visit somewhere near a lake, river, or ocean, take this book with you. Look around carefully and record everything you find that is mentioned in this book. Take a photograph if you can. You can also record other interesting things that are not in this book. Look up these new things on the Internet and write your own descriptions.

Here are some questions you could ask yourself:

1 What is it?

2 Where did I see it?

3 When did I see it?

4 What was it doing?

5 What interesting information did my research uncover?

Glossary

amphipod (AMP-fih-pod)
A small, shrimplike
marine animal.

barrier island
(BER-ee-er EYE-lund)
A narrow strip of sand usually
running parallel to the coast.

blowhole (BLOH-hohl)
The hole in the roof of a sea
cave that emits large
quantities of water depending
on wave action.

crustacean
(krus-TAY-shun) A marine
animal that has no backbone,
but a hard shell instead, such
as a lobster, shrimp, and crab.

foredunes (FOR-doonz)
Sand dunes immediately next
to the beach.

lagoon (luh-GOON) A body
of water separated from
the main body by a sand or
coral bar.

mollusks (MAH-lusks)
Animals, such as oysters and
mussels, with soft bodies
usually enclosed by shells.

neap tide (NEEP TYD)
A tide with a small range
between low and high tide,
occurring during quarter-
moon phases.

photosynthesis
(foh-toh-SIN-thuh-sus)
The process by which plants
produce energy from carbon
dioxide and sunlight.

plankton (PLANK-ten)
Minute plant and animal
life that drifts in oceans
and lakes.

river delta
(RIH-ver DEL-tuh) Land that
forms in the mouth of a river
where it flows into a large
body of water.

sea stacks (SEE STAKS)
Small, vertical-sided islands
situated in the ocean just
off shore.

spit (SPIT) A narrow strip of
land connected to the
mainland at one end only.

spring tide (SPRING TYD)
A tide with the greatest range
between low and high tide,
occurring during a full or
new moon.

storm surge (STORM
SURJ) A rise in the sea level
caused by bad weather.

tombolo (TOHM-buh-loh)
A strip of sand or gravel
that joins an island to
the mainland.

zooxanthellae
(zoh-uh-zan-THEH-luh)
Tiny plants that depend on
coral for their existence and,
in return, provide coral with a
food source.

Index

Websites

Due to the changing nature of Internet links, PowerKids Press has developed an online list of websites related to the subject of this book. This site is updated regularly. Please use this link to access the list: www.powerkidslinks.com/disc/coast/